Behind the Silence

Discovering the Colors of the Autistic World

Copyright

Behind the Silence
Discovering the Colors of the Autistic World

DISCLAIMER AND TERMS OF USE

(Please read before using this report)

This information is not provided by a doctor and is for informational purposes only. This content should never replace a doctor's opinion, diagnosis or professional treatment. Before making any decision, consult a doctor.

Always seek the advice of your doctor or other health professional if you have any doubts about a medical condition. Always follow professional medical advice and don't delay in seeing a doctor based on what you've read.

Natural and dietary supplements are not approved by Anvisa. For this reason, they must include a disclaimer on the product label. This statement should make it clear that Anvisa has not evaluated the product and that it is not intended to diagnose, treat, cure or prevent any disease.

The author and publisher shall not be liable under any circumstances for any direct, indirect, punitive, special, incidental or other damages arising from the use of this material.

As always, it is important to seek the help of a qualified legal, tax, accounting, medical or other professional. The author does not guarantee the performance, effectiveness or applicability of any sites listed or linked to in this course.

CONTENTS

Chapter 1 - What causes autism

When a doctor tells parents that their child has Autism, the first question that comes up is: How did this happen? How did my child get this disease?

Well, there is no definitive answer to what the exact causes of autism are. However, there are several ideas that researchers and doctors are working on. It has been discovered that autism is more common in boys than in girls.

In the past, it was believed that autism was caused by emotional trauma. In other words, parental behavior could be one of the causes. Doctors said that mothers who didn't give their children enough attention and love were the problem. But with further studies and research, these factors were found to be wrong. The best-known theory about the causes of autism is genetic.

Some researchers believe that people are born with a tendency to have autism. Then certain triggers in their environment make them autistic. They say there are several genes related to autism, but they haven't found them yet.

Environmental factors are also considered to be an important cause of autism. Studies show that there are many cases of autism in small towns that are exposed to high levels of toxins and chemicals.

Usually, cities near industrial areas or factories have very toxic air that can cause autism in children. Another interesting theory about autism is related to mercury.

Some say that since autism was first diagnosed at almost the same time as the vaccines were given, it may have been caused by the mercury in the vaccines. Currently, vaccines have almost zero or harmless amounts of mercury for the human body.

Besides, there's no reason to blame vaccines. In fact, failing to vaccinate can lead to other serious risks for the child. Therefore, you shouldn't avoid vaccinations thinking that they can prevent autism.

Research indicates that there may be a certain link between pregnant mothers and their children with autism.

Researchers are currently testing the amount of mercury in pregnant women and studying the babies at birth. This would help to monitor whether the theory is true or not. In addition, autism is linked to some hidden health problems. Children with conditions such as Fragile X Syndrome and Congenital Rubella are said to be more likely to have autism. Metabolic imbalance is also said to be a factor. Researchers say that metabolic imbalance in children can also lead to autism. To better understand the cause of autism, more studies and analysis are needed. I hope that one day we will be able to prevent and treat this disease.

Until then, we must face it with courage.

Chapter 2 - Accepting the diagnosis of autism

When you find out that your child has autism, it's natural to feel afraid, lonely and overwhelmed. But you don't have to feel terrified. There are many organizations and people ready to help you through this journey. When dealing with an autism diagnosis, it's common to go through different emotional stages. Here are the stages you are likely to go through:

Stage 1 - Denial: It's normal to deny the diagnosis at first. You may think that the doctors are wrong. It's good to seek a second opinion, but if the second opinion confirms autism, there's no point in continuing to look for a different answer. It's important to get through this phase so that you can accept the diagnosis and start treatment as soon as possible.

Stage 2 - Anger: Feeling angry is natural. You may feel angry with yourself, wondering if you've done something wrong. You may feel angry at God, wondering why your child has autism. It's also possible to feel angry at other parents with healthy children, wondering why they don't have to deal with autism. It's important to talk to someone you trust about these feelings, such as a doctor or a counselor.

Stage 3 - Grief: Feeling sad is normal when you receive difficult news. Don't blame yourself for feeling heartbroken. However, don't let this sadness consume you, as it could affect your child and make them feel guilty. It's important to work through grief, but it's also a natural process. If you find that you are grieving for too long or if the people around you believe that you are taking too long, seek the help of a counselor.

Stage 4 - Acceptance: It can take time to reach this stage, but it is the ultimate goal when dealing with an autism diagnosis. At this point, you can move on and seek the best care for your child. Your child is different, but that's not a bad thing, and you should never feel that way. When you finally accept the diagnosis of autism, you and your child can move on and have a happy life. Autism doesn't change that.

Managing autism can be challenging, depending on the severity of the case. There are services available to help you, so you never feel overwhelmed. If you spend a lot of time in any of the early stages, it is recommended that you seek counseling, as experts in this type of situation can help you move forward.

It is important for parents to accept their child's autism, both for their own sake and for the sake of the child. The only way to really help your child is to accept reality and move on in their life journey.

Chapter 3 - Doctors and Autism Diagnosis

Receiving a diagnosis of autism for your child can be painful. It's natural to consider a second opinion, and you have every right to do so. However, once the diagnosis is confirmed, it's important to start treatment.

If you suspect your child may have autism, look out for some signs. If you notice speech problems or a delay in speech compared to other children of the same age, this is cause for concern.

Also observe how your child interacts with other children. If they avoid playing with others or don't feel comfortable in social environments, it's a good idea to see a doctor for more information.

If a doctor suspects a problem, he or she will carry out a series of tests. Each child is unique, so a single test is not enough to diagnose autism.

Children show symptoms and respond to the disorder in different ways. The doctor will carry out a full assessment, including a family history. If autism is suspected, he or she may refer you to a specialist in autism and similar disorders for a proper diagnosis.

The doctor will start the process with hearing tests. Hearing problems can be one of the reasons why your child doesn't speak well or has difficulties interacting. There are two ways to carry out the hearing test.

The first is done while the child is awake and reacts to sounds. The second is done while the child is sedated and a machine measures brain activity in response to certain sounds.

Blood and urine tests can also be carried out to analyze the DNA. The doctor may be looking for Fragile X Syndrome, which often occurs in children with autism.

In addition to DNA tests, the doctor may order an MRI or CT scan to examine brain function. If the diagnosis of autism is confirmed, it's important to provide your child with structure and support, starting with the doctor.

Avoid seeing several doctors in the hope of getting a different diagnosis. Look for a doctor who offers consistent treatment for your child, preferably with the same medical team. Always being seen by the same professional will help your child develop trust, as they will see a familiar face at each visit.

Chapter 4 - Signs of Autism

As parents seek to understand autism, it is important to be aware of the symptoms of this condition. As doctors explain, the earlier autism is diagnosed, the greater the chances of a better life for the child and their family. Below is a list of symptoms of autism. This list is not exhaustive, but if you notice any of these signs in your child, it is advisable to consult a doctor. An assessment and a check-up can help start the right treatment and significantly improve the child's life.

1. The child doesn't reach developmental milestones. While some children start crawling at around 4 months, others may take longer.

Although there is no fixed deadline for reaching these milestones, if the child is late in reaching them, it is important to check with a doctor.

2. Your child doesn't speak. As children develop, they begin to make sounds and eventually speak words and complete sentences. Generally, around the age of 16 months, children begin to babble a few words. If your child isn't talking at all after this age, it's a cause for concern and may require further medical evaluation.

3. The child avoids eye contact. Babies and children often make eye contact while interacting with other people. However, children with autism tend to avoid eye contact. They seem to be lost in their own world and don't look

directly at others. If you notice this lack of eye contact, it is recommended that you consult a doctor.

4. Lack of emotional expression. Children with autism may have difficulty showing emotions. They may not smile back when someone smiles at them and they may not react emotionally to situations that usually provoke reactions in typical children. In addition, they may avoid hugs or displays of affection.

5. Preference for being alone. Children with autism often prefer to play alone rather than interact with other children. They may have difficulty making friends and may not understand jokes or figures of speech. They may also

interpret words literally, without understanding the figurative meaning.

6. Difficulty retaining information. Autistic children can have difficulty retaining what they are taught. They may forget basic skills and tasks that have been taught previously and need constant reminding.

These are just some of the signs of autism. It is important to note that not all children with autism will show all the signs mentioned. They may only exhibit one or a few of them. If you observe any of these signs in your child, it is recommended that you consult a doctor for a proper assessment.

Remember that the sooner the diagnosis is made, the sooner treatment can begin. Even if you don't think there's anything wrong with your child, it's always safer to have them assessed to make sure everything is fine.

Chapter 5 - Gluten-free diet

Gluten is a protein found in many of the foods we eat every day. But for children with autism, the body reacts differently from normal.

That's why it's important for parents to plan a gluten-free diet for their autistic children. This diet is not a cure for autism, but it can help reduce symptoms. However, it is necessary to follow the diet for several months, not just a few weeks, to see results.

It takes time to notice the effects of the gluten-free diet. The body needs time to get rid of the gluten that has already been consumed. In some cases, however, people notice immediate improvements.

Following a gluten-free diet requires planning. Foods such as rye, wheat and barley contain a lot of gluten, so they are also present in most breads. But there are other grains that don't contain gluten, such as brown rice, corn, buckwheat, millet, amaranth, quinoa, oats, soybeans and sunflower seeds.

Sometimes vinegars, sauces and even spices can contain gluten. In addition, many snacks and cookies contain gluten. It is important to read food labels during the gluten-free diet.

Following a gluten-free diet can be more expensive, as these foods are usually sold in stores specializing in health or natural products. However, nowadays, many supermarkets also carry these products.

There are gluten-free options such as flour, pancake mix, waffles, cookies and snacks. One tip is for parents to get together to buy in bulk, which reduces costs and allows families to share food.

Cooking at home is also an economical option for the gluten-free diet. There are recipes available on the internet, in cookbooks and you can also get information from a nutritionist.

Children with autism can eat meat, fruit, fish, vegetables, eggs, nuts and other gluten-free foods. To make the diet more interesting for the child, you can prepare fun snacks using gluten-free ingredients, such as muffins and cookies. Once this practice becomes part of the family routine, it will be easier to follow.

Many autistic children are also allergic to the casein found in dairy products. For this reason, many people reduce or eliminate dairy products when following this diet. However, it is important to test your child for allergies. Your doctor and nutritionist can give you more advice.

Remember that the gluten- and casein-free diet is not a cure for autism. However, many parents who have adopted it have noticed improvements in their children's health.

Chapter 6 - Treatments for Autism

When starting a treatment plan for an autistic person, doctors look at different treatment options that can help. As each autistic person has different symptoms, the treatment plan is personalized for each individual. There is no single treatment that cures autism, but there are solutions that can reduce symptoms and help people lead a fully functional life.

It's understandable that parents don't want to start their child on medication straight away when there's a diagnosis of autism. There are other options to consider. Alternative treatments include changes to the child's diet or the use of natural treatments.

The child's education is an extremely important aspect. Teachers and educators must be willing to adapt lessons to the needs of the autistic child. This may involve revising lesson plans or incorporating certain specific aspects into lessons. Unfortunately, there is no single treatment that works for all people with autism.

Usually, treatment plans involve different approaches, including self-education, proper diet, positive reinforcement and, in some cases, medication. Let's take a look at the types of medication an autistic person might need to take:

Antipsychotics: These are used to treat behavioral problems such as aggression, tantrums or insomnia. However, this should not be the first treatment option for the child. Behavioral therapy should be tried before resorting to these drugs.

Anticonvulsants: These are used to control seizures in autistic people who suffer from them.

Medications for anxiety and depression: Autistic children have difficulty controlling their emotions and may laugh or cry for no apparent reason. These drugs help control these emotional outbursts. However, they can have serious side effects. If your child is taking these drugs, keep an eye out for strange behavioral changes that were not present before treatment.

Sedatives: If your autistic child has problems with insomnia or other sleep disorders, a doctor may prescribe a sedative to help them sleep better. Before trying sedatives, there are natural alternatives you can consider.

Stimulants: Some autistic children are hyperactive and these drugs are used to help them concentrate better. This is often used when the child is of school age, to help them pay attention and perform better academically. This option is useful for children who have difficulty concentrating in certain areas. However, medication should be the last resort for parents when treating their children, to avoid addiction.

It's important to remember that these solutions can control problems, but they can also cause side effects that lead to new problems. Talk to your doctor if you notice that the medication isn't helping. He or she may suggest other medication alternatives or even a different treatment.

Maintain good communication with your child's doctor, as this will greatly help to adjust the treatment whenever necessary.

Chapter 7 - Different treatments for autism

As more research is done into autism, a problem in brain development, doctors and researchers are finding different ways to treat it. Medication is usually the only option, but it can have unpleasant side effects. Parents are looking for natural ways to treat their autistic children.

There are some alternative methods of treating autism that are more common than others. Some are used alone, while others are combined. It is not known which method works best for each child. Talk to a doctor to find out about different treatments for autistic children. Here are some tips:

Music therapy: Autistic children have responded to music in various ways. Sometimes the music makes them happy and they want to move, which helps with their movements. Other times, the children sing along with the words of the song, helping with their speech. This has also been seen in children who don't even speak. Music therapy is a natural way to help autistic children.

Sensory Integration: Everyone, whether autistic or not, has a smell that reminds them of something happy. Or the touch of a specific fabric evokes special feelings. This is also true for some autistic children. Researchers have used sensory skills to make autistic children react. Autistic children rely more on hearing, touch, taste and smell to understand and communicate. This is also used to calm autistic children with the use of specific smells or textures.

Nutrition: An autistic child's diet can affect how they react. There are many different diets that doctors have used. Some of the popular diets are gluten-free, i.e. without wheat products, or removing dairy products from the diet. Certain ingredients in food can cause an autistic person to have negative behaviors or reactions. Find out what these ingredients are and remove them from your child's diet.

Omega 3: Omega 3 is a healthy fat that brings health benefits. These benefits include better sleep patterns, improved social skills and better general health. All of these aspects are positive for a child with autism. Although it is possible to buy Omega 3 in many supplement stores, discuss with your doctor the benefits of trying Omega 3 in your autistic child's diet. Omega 3 and other essential fats are necessary for a child's normal growth. However, there have been no major studies on the benefits of fish oil for autistic children.

Play therapy: Play as a form of therapy is effective because it doesn't feel like hard work. Children with autism feel more relaxed in a play environment and have the opportunity to express themselves naturally. When a therapist starts playing with the autistic child, both the therapist and the child have a chance to connect. Through play, the child develops trust in the therapist, facilitating the therapy sessions. By strengthening these bonds through play, autistic children also learn to play appropriately with other children of the same age.

Good treatment plans can include some of these alternatives, along with the solutions recommended by your doctor. You can also try these alternatives before resorting to medication.

It's important to remember that every child is different, so some alternative therapies may work well for one autistic child but not for another. Don't be discouraged if one approach doesn't work for your child. Look for ways to keep your child happy while providing the best possible care.

Chapter 8 - How to act as parents of an autistic child

Being a parent of an autistic child requires courage, patience and optimism. Although it's rewarding when things are smooth, sometimes you need time to deal with the stress and vent your frustrations.

It's important to understand that your frustrations, stress and sadness can harm your child. To be a successful father, you need to be happy and determined, as this also influences your child's happiness.

Here are some ways you can help during your journey with your autistic child.

Support groups: Joining local support groups is a way of talking and sharing problems with other people going through the same situation. They can offer unexpected suggestions and solutions for the child's daily routine and activities. It's also an opportunity to meet other people, listen to their experiences and learn from them. It also provides a break from therapists and doctors.

Journaling: Expressing your feelings and thoughts in writing can be a great way to relax emotionally. Keep the diary private. This activity helps you get to know yourself better and observe your child's behavior on a daily basis.

Time for yourself: We all need moments of rest, where we can be alone or with our partner. There are activities that cannot be done with children, whether they are autistic or not. Find a qualified caregiver for your child and go out for a date night with your partner. Do activities you've always wanted to, such as watching your favorite movie, playing sports or interesting games. If you can't leave the house, enjoy a relaxing bath after your child goes to sleep. Pamper yourself and do things you enjoy. This will relieve stress and help you to be a better parent.

Ask for help: We want to give the best to our children, but sometimes we forget that our frustration and anger affect the child. It's okay to ask for help. Unless we communicate our problems and ask for help, no one will know how to help, because people can't read our thoughts.

Being a parent of an autistic child definitely requires help. If you're trying a treatment that isn't working, talk to someone and ask for guidance.

Convincing an autistic child to do certain tasks can be difficult. At such times, having someone to help with simple tasks makes things easier. Seek help from your partner and talk about your problems with them, as this makes a difference. Managing life with an autistic child can be challenging, so it's important to act carefully at every step.

Stay calm and try to reduce stress in simple ways to be a successful parent for your child.

Chapter 9 - Allowing your autistic child to be a child

As parents of an autistic child, we sometimes forget that their lives need more than doctors and therapists. We get so protective and worried about every little detail that we don't give them time to be children.

It's important to allow them time to do what they want. Here are some things that are sure to make your child happy.

Let your autistic child choose their favorite activities or games during a certain time of the day. This could be playing with their favorite toys or taking up a hobby such as drawing or painting. This gives your child a break from medical appointments and therapies.

Plan special activities for your autistic child, such as dinner at their favorite restaurant or a picnic in a nearby park. These activities can be planned once a week. Sometimes your child might also like to spend time with their grandparents.

If you protect your child too much and don't allow them to join in with the other children, they may develop fears and insecurities. Let them run, jump and shout like the other children. Children love to get dirty and have fun like that. Allow your child to get dirty, it won't hurt as much as you think. A bath can wash away the dirt and they'll have their share of fun.

Being autistic doesn't mean that your child can't lead a normal life. Teach them to be brave and to achieve their dreams. Their condition should not be an obstacle in any way.

At this stage of life, children often use excuses to get special treatment. Don't let autism be an excuse for your child. Punishing them for their mistakes and making them face the consequences will help make them strong and prepared for adult life.

Give your child simple tasks to do as part of their daily activities, such as making their bed or preparing their backpack for school. Make sure the child is capable of doing the task and praise them when they do it correctly. This will boost their confidence and give them a sense of achievement.

Encourage your child to do their best in all areas of life and show them that you have expectations for them. If they are not challenged to use their full potential, they will never discover their true strength.

Playing in the mud, getting dirty, slipping and falling while smiling are all things children love to do. Playing with their favorite toy and screaming with joy is fun for them. Don't be overprotective, be a guide and allow your child to be free at times. Even if they have special needs, they will be much happier as a child who is free to choose the activities they enjoy doing of their own free will.

Chapter 10 - Children with autism need timetables

Children of all ages, from 3 to 13, often feel bored. When you ask them to do something, they don't do it, and this can be very difficult. That's why, especially in the case of autistic children, having an agenda is very helpful.

As parents, we need to organize our children's school schedules, therapies, doctor's appointments, homework and daily chores well. Your child's health and growth must be the priority in all of this.

Having an agenda creates a defined structure for the child. They know what to expect, for example, what they will be doing tomorrow and at what time.

Children with autism often face anxiety problems.

When they are left free to think without guidance, they can have very sad thoughts. A well-organized schedule leaves less or no free time, which greatly reduces anxiety. This avoids interruptions to necessary tasks and medical procedures.

Getting them to do something important that they don't like, like finishing their homework, is made easier with an agenda. You make them switch to "the task of studying and doing homework" after finishing the previous "task". Then you can direct the child to the next task. This other "activity" may be more interesting for the child, such as "drawing" or "playing outside".

With multiple appointments, therapies and medical needs, managing your child's schedule can be tricky. It's easy to forget an appointment with the therapist or doctor. An agenda helps you keep track of each appointment without fail. Once you've created an agenda for your child, show it to them in a visual way, with an attractive graphic in their personal space or bedroom.

Allow them to follow the steps on their own, of course with your guidance. This will increase their self-confidence and decision-making skills. Sometimes autistic children have difficulty reading words.

This is where the "Visual Timetable" system comes in, where each task or activity is represented by a symbol or drawing. For example, you could use a garden to represent outdoor games, a pile of books for studying, a stethoscope for a doctor's appointment and a handshake for therapy sessions. If there are any changes to the timetable, explain them to your child in advance and in detail. As the child will be planning their activities according to the schedule, even a small change can upset them. Therefore, involve them in the decision to make the change, so that they feel more independent and confident.

In our day-to-day lives, it can be difficult to keep to set times, but it's important to try to do so as much as possible. For example, if your child usually wakes up at 7 a.m., it's a good idea to keep to this schedule at weekends too.

Likewise, it is advisable to avoid large variations in bedtimes, as adequate sleep contributes to your child's health. By following this advice from the experts, as a parent you will certainly notice improvements in your child's behavior with set schedules. Having an established routine makes your life much easier and allows you to manage it more smoothly.

Chapter 11 - Ten tips for enjoying the vacations with your autistic child

The vacations are a time for excitement, celebration, festivities and spending time with family. This may sound very exciting for us, but it can be tedious and overwhelming for an autistic child. Does this mean that parents of an autistic child can no longer enjoy the vacations? Not at all!

With a few precautions and tips, you can have a wonderful vacation with your family and your autistic child. Here are a few things to remember:

1. Take shorter breaks. Less time means not overloading the child with tiring activities. Too many emotions and

excitement can be difficult for an autistic child. Shorter time-outs will help to balance them out and prevent tiredness.

2. Let your child choose the activities. If they don't want to take part in an activity, don't force them. For example, when everyone is having dinner at the table, your child may prefer to eat in a quiet place. Leave them to it.

3. Try to maintain the daily routine as much as possible. If your child is used to going to bed at 8pm, don't force them to stay up late. If that's not possible, try to get them to take a nap. Nobody likes dealing with an irritable, sleepy child, not even their family.

4. Spread the activities over a few days. It's not necessary to visit all the relatives in one day. Remember that an autistic child can feel overwhelmed by too many people at once. Give them time and breaks so that they can enjoy the family reunion without getting stressed. The family will also be happy to meet your child when they are well.

5. Avoid long shopping sessions with your child. The crowds in shopping malls and markets during Christmas can be annoying even for adults, so imagine how your autistic child would feel. In addition, unfamiliar surroundings can make an autistic child uncomfortable. Consider hiring a reliable babysitter to stay at home with your child. If this is not possible, leave your child with your spouse or another

responsible family member. Dealing with your child in these situations can be challenging for you as a parent.

6. Don't open all the presents at once. Children love presents, but the excitement of opening several at once can be too intense for an autistic child. Open one present at a time, giving your child time to enjoy and get used to the festivities. Let them open presents little by little, spaced out over a few days.

7. Don't change your child's diet just for fun. If your child is following a special diet plan, stand firm and prevent other family members from offering restricted foods. Even if some people disagree with the effectiveness of the diet plan, stand by your decision and

follow your beliefs for the benefit of your child.

8. Have fun with your child during the vacations and include them in family activities. Don't exclude them from the group. Be optimistic and pass on this optimism to your child, thanking God for everything in life.

9. Reward your child for good behavior during outings. Children love challenges and rewards. Recognize and reward your child for behaving well while with the family. This will make them feel a sense of accomplishment and will encourage proper behavior and prevent any mischief.

10. Be patient when your child is stressed or anxious. Being a parent of

an autistic child requires planning and patience when traveling.

However, during the vacations, try to put aside the worries of the daily routine and really enjoy the time with your child. Your stress and agitation will only increase your child's anxiety and stress. Be grateful for the good things in life and allow your mind and heart to relax.

Chapter 12 - Treatments for Asperger's Syndrome

Asperger's Syndrome is a type of autism that affects the way people socialize and communicate. It can also cause difficulties with motor skills. Treatment for Asperger's Syndrome varies from child to child.

There are no drugs to treat Asperger's Syndrome, but there are treatments that can help with the symptoms. These treatments vary because what works for one child may not work for another.

Here are some types of treatment that a child with Asperger's Syndrome can receive:

- Social skills training: Children with Asperger's Syndrome have difficulty understanding facial expressions and tone of voice. They may have difficulty noticing when someone is making jokes or being sarcastic. This training helps children recognize and understand these differences. It also helps them to make eye contact and interact better with other people.

- Cognitive-behavioral therapy: This therapy helps children deal with difficult situations and reduce stress and anxiety. It also teaches strategies for dealing with angry outbursts and emotional breakdowns.

- Parental education: Parents and other family members can also learn how to deal with children who have Asperger's

Syndrome. One example is the use of a reward system, where the child is encouraged to calm down and behave well. Parents also learn how to deal with angry outbursts.

- Medical treatments: There is no cure for Asperger's Syndrome, but some medication can be prescribed to treat symptoms such as anxiety, depression and sleeping difficulties. It is important to closely monitor the child's response to treatment and observe their behavior.

- Positive reinforcement: Children with Asperger's Syndrome respond well when they are praised and encouraged by their parents and other authority figures. Showing them what they need to do and supporting them in their efforts helps to promote their independence.

It's important to remember that there is no magic solution or treatment that will completely cure Asperger's Syndrome, but there are ways to help reduce the symptoms. Talk to your doctor about the treatment options available to help your child adapt to social environments.

Chapter 13 - What is Global Development Disorder?

Global Developmental Disorder (GDD) is a diagnosis given to children who show some, but not all, signs of autism.

TGD is usually diagnosed in children, but can be identified earlier. Children with developmental delays are screened for autism, but may be diagnosed with Global Developmental Disorder, which is a milder form of autism.

Children with this disorder can show different symptoms. As all children develop at different rates, symptoms can vary from one child to another. They may have difficulties in social interaction and problems communicating with parents and peers, which are two of the problems that children with this disorder can face.

When a child has social skills delays, this can be observed from an early age. For example, babies may not make eye contact or respond to affection. This can be challenging for parents, and it's important to talk to your doctor if you notice any of these problems.

As children grow up, they may prefer to play alone and have no problem not interacting with other children of the same age. They may have no difficulty separating from their parents or talking to strangers.

Children with a milder form of this disorder can have social difficulties in different ways. Some children want to have friends, but find it difficult to make them because of their social problems.

As children get older, they tend to get closer to their parents and other people who are always around, but find it difficult to make new friends and interact with strangers. Speech and communication can also be a challenge for some children with Global Developmental Disorder.

Unfortunately, these problems may not be noticed until the child is older. As babies, they may not babble, and parents may even consider it a blessing that they don't have to deal with a noisy baby.

However, as they grow up, they don't start speaking. Sometimes they pick up a word and just repeat it, without learning new words. There are more difficulties than just learning to speak.

Children with the disorder may have difficulty learning new words and also understanding facial expressions and voice intonations. They may not realize when someone is joking or being sarcastic, interpreting everything literally. It is important that they learn to differentiate between these issues.

Another common problem in people with this disorder is an excessive interest in a particular subject, talking about it repeatedly and not addressing other topics. Expressing emotions can also be difficult for these children. They tend to be emotionally indifferent most of the time, but when they do show emotions, it is usually in an intense way.

These children can have outbursts and show fits of anger, but they can also express sadness, happiness and fear. They can express any emotion.

These are two of the main symptoms observed in children with a global development disorder. If you notice any of these symptoms, it's important to consult a doctor for a more detailed assessment.

Chapter 14 - Signs of Global Development Disorder

Global Developmental Disorder is less severe than autism. Children who have some developmental difficulties can be diagnosed with this disorder (GDD). Some of them don't have all the symptoms of autism.

Children with Global Developmental Disorder will show different symptoms from one another, because each child's problem will be different. Children grow and develop in different ways, and children with this problem are no exception.

Some signs of TGD are not common. There are several behaviors in this category. Your child may have repetitive actions. They want to do the same thing all the time, eat the same food or keep doing the same action over and over again. This can include clapping their hands or twirling their fingers.

In addition, children with this disorder like routine. They want to do the same thing at the same time every day. They don't like it when their routine changes. If this happens, they may have an outburst or a fit of rage which is not a normal reaction to the situation.

They may organize their room in a certain way, and if someone moves things around, they can get very angry. Some children will become obsessed with a certain object or subject. For example, if they like airplanes, they might learn everything they can about them. They will have pictures of airplanes and look at them in the sky. These obsessive behaviors usually only happen with one thing, and the child won't care much about other things.

Learning a new skill is difficult for these children. Their developmental skills are challenging. This can include things like using the potty or toilet, brushing their teeth or combing their hair. Because they are so used to routine and always do the same thing, having to learn something new will change their lifestyle.

Some children with Global Developmental Disorder have sensory problems. They can become attached to a certain fabric or a specific blanket. A piece of clothing or even a smell can soothe the child.

They'll take it everywhere, as if they never want to part with it. Often, they will like things with the same texture and smell too. However, sounds have the opposite effect: they don't like high-pitched sounds. When they hear something loud, they can get nervous.

Your child may not want to be hugged. They may not want to be touched unless they are playing. This is not common in children and should be checked if this is the case. These behaviors could be caused by other problems in your child. If you observe any of these behaviors, talk to your doctor.

Unusual behavior is also just one symptom. There may be other symptoms that your child will show if they have this disorder.

Chapter 15 - Diagnosis of Global Development Disorder

A doctor will look at a list of criteria to determine whether your child has this disorder. Assessments will be made in several areas.

Medical assessment: The doctor will order various tests, including hearing, blood and urine tests. If there are any health problems, the doctor will also carry out a physical examination to check for other problems.

Educational Assessment: The doctor will check your child's level of knowledge based on what is expected for their school age. Various areas will be checked, such as dressing, bathing, social interaction and other skills. This can be assessed through interviews with parents, teachers and other people close to the child. It is also useful to keep a diary of everything your child does and how they react in order to help the doctor.

Psychological assessment: A psychologist will interview the child to see if they have any mental disorders. Some of the symptoms your child has may be caused by other conditions, and the doctor will want to rule out these possibilities.

Behavioral observation: The doctor may want to observe your child in their natural environment. By observing the child, the doctor will be able to assess their behavior. They will be able to see first-hand how the child interacts with other children of the same age and at home.

Communication Assessment: The doctor will test the child's communication skills. This is important to determine whether the child has autism or some other developmental problem. Communication can occur in various ways, not just through words. The doctor will assess body language, facial expressions and other forms of communication.

Occupational Assessment: The child's motor skills are important in determining whether they have autism. Tests will be carried out to check the child's motor skills and senses. They may have an aversion to certain textures or smells. This is important to identify what is happening to the child.

Many of these assessments are made during interviews with parents, teachers or anyone close to the child. A child can show different symptoms at different times.

That's why it's important to get as much information as possible from people who can help, so don't hesitate to seek help. Once the assessments have been completed, the doctor or pediatrician will consult other specialists to make a diagnosis. The doctors will then decide whether the child has autism or a Global Developmental Disorder.

Once your child has been diagnosed, a treatment plan will be provided. This will help your child lead a normal life and communicate better with people. Getting a diagnosis is the first step towards helping your child lead a better life.

Conclusion

In conclusion, it's imperative to understand that autism is not a barrier to happiness or familial harmony; rather, it's a unique aspect of a person's identity. By embracing this perspective, parents can cultivate an environment of acceptance, support, and love within their family. While the journey may present challenges, it also offers moments of profound growth, understanding, and joy. By fostering open communication, seeking out resources, and celebrating the individual strengths and talents of their autistic child, families can forge a path towards a fulfilling and enriching life together. Ultimately, the bond of love transcends any diagnosis, empowering families to navigate the complexities of autism with resilience, compassion, and hope.

Dear reader,

We want to thank you for having come this far. Visit our website www.ebooktop.com.br register and contribute your suggestions, criticisms or compliments.

Thank you very much!